MASKS

Devotions of Hope for the Downcast

TERRY BUETHE

Copyright © 2014 by Terry Buethe

MASKS
Devotions of Hope for the Downcast
by Terry Buethe

Printed in the United States of America

ISBN 9781498411134

All rights reserved solely by the author. The author guarantees all contents are original and do not infringe upon the legal rights of any other person or work. No part of this book may be reproduced in any form without the permission of the author. The views expressed in this book are not necessarily those of the publisher.

Scripture quotations taken from The Holy Bible, English Standard Version (ESV). Copyright © 2001 by Crossway, a publishing ministry of Good News Publishers. Used by permission. All rights reserved.

www.xulonpress.com

TABLE OF CONTENTS

Introduction v
A Note About Depression ix
Acknowledgements xi
Endorsement xiii

1. A Double-Edged Sword 15
2. So Many Voices 17
3. The Ultimate Mask 19
4. Who Am I? 21
5. Successful or Faithful? 23
6. Rest in Peace 26
7. What Are You Afraid Of? 29
8. Nobody Wants Me 31
9. Swallowing Your Pride 33
10. Re-Learning to Receive 36
11. First Things Second, or Third, or… 39
12. Why Does It Hurt So Much? 42
13. Follow Your Heart? 45
14. I Need to be Strong 48
15. Losing Some Weight 51
16. I Can't Do Anything Right! 53
17. Do, Be, Do, Be, Do? 56
18. Eve Syndrome 58
19. Guilt 60
20. It's Not Fair! 63
21. Where Do I Belong? 65

22. Starting Over 67
23. Great Expectations 69
24. What Are You Worth? 72
25. Through the Looking Glass 75
26. HELP!! 78
27. What if...?. 81
28. Urgent or Important? 83
29. Quicksand 86
30. What's the Word? 88

Devotional Thoughts. 91
About the Author 101
End Notes. 103

INTRODUCTION

The masks of life. We all have them and use them. It's part of being "civilized," or at least civil. We wear a mask while dealing with that irritating coworker or overbearing relative because if we acted the way we truly felt there would be consequences. So masks serve a vital purpose for coexisting with other human beings.

But for some, masks are more than just temporary coping tools. For people living and growing up in homes where drugs or alcohol are abused or where family members are abused (regardless of the type of abuse), masks become a survival tool. Wearing a mask over one's true feelings becomes a continual part of daily existence.

Masks are also used to hide other types of pain–loneliness, failure, anger, shame, grief and many others. Sometimes it's just easier to deal with the world when those emotions can be hidden away from the people encountered on the journey through the days, weeks, months and even years of life.

The downside of wearing a mask so much of the time is that the real self can get lost. Losing track of what constitutes the mask and what is one's true identity becomes an increasing possibility. Perpetual mask-wearers can reach the point of asking, "Is this who I really am?"

Masks can also isolate a person from others because they don't let people know the real us. Masks make it difficult for others, even those closest to us, to know what we are going through and how we are feeling. Masks can even put distance between us and our heavenly Father. Not because God has moved farther from us, but because by using masks we push ourselves away from Him. While our masks can help us feel safe, they can also isolate us, feeding those feelings of loneliness.

These devotions are intended to help sort out some of these issues of identity and the effects of masks. They will help you consider who you are in light of your relationship with God and with those He has placed in your life. They will also examine some "masks" that are beneficial and even assigned to us by our Creator and Lord.

May God bless your time in these devotions with a better understanding of your identity in Christ and your relationship with Him.

Baptismal Identity

Identifying yourself as a baptized child of God is foundational to many of these devotions. God works through His Word combined with the water of baptism to do marvelous things. In baptism, He puts His name on you. The act of baptism is a pronouncement of God's Triune name as the water is applied to the candidate. This naming is an act of adoption as God makes you His child and brings you into His family.

Through baptism you are joined with Christ. We are told in Romans 6: "Do you not know that all of us who have been baptized into Christ Jesus were baptized into his death?" (v.3) Through this union you receive all the benefits of Christ's death and resurrection, freedom from the eternal consequences of your sins and the promise of your own resurrection.

Baptism also washes away your sins, or in other words it delivers the forgiveness Christ won for you on the cross. "And now why do you wait? Rise and be baptized and wash away your sins, calling on his name." (Acts 22:16) Through baptism you receive the Holy Spirit (Acts 2:38) and thus saving faith is created, faith necessary for trusting Jesus Christ as your Lord and Savior and receiving forgiveness.

Through the miraculous gift of baptism God unites all believers into one body, the body of Christ. (1 Cor 12:13) Christ's body is the Church and it is there that God promises to deliver His grace through Word and Sacrament to all who come before Him in repentance.

Holding to these biblical teachings of baptism lays a deep and broad foundation to carry us through our days in this fallen world. Secure on that foundation, we can live in peace and hope even in the face of trials.

A NOTE ABOUT DEPRESSION

According to a World Health Organization flyer, depression is the leading cause of disability worldwide.[1] In a recently published article, the Center for Disease Control reported 8% of Americans age twelve or over are reporting depression at any given time. For men the depression rate is 7% while women have a 12% rate.[2]

Dealing with clinical depression is not typically a self-help situation. It often requires counseling and/or medication to stabilize moods and get one's internal dialog back on track. For many this type of intervention is short-term, lasting only until circumstances are back in a more normal balance. But for some medical or mental health intervention is a long-term prospect. Only a professional mental health practitioner can properly diagnose and treat clinical depression.

According to the Mayo Clinic web site:

Although depression may occur only one time during your life, usually people have multiple episodes of depression. During these episodes, symptoms occur most of the day, nearly every day and may include:

- *Feelings of sadness, emptiness or unhappiness*

- *Angry outbursts, irritability or frustration, even over small matters*
- *Loss of interest or pleasure in normal activities, such as sex*
- *Sleep disturbances, including insomnia or sleeping too much*
- *Tiredness and lack of energy, so that even small tasks take extra effort*
- *Changes in appetite—often reduced appetite and weight loss, but increased cravings for food and weight gain in some people*
- *Anxiety, agitation or restlessness—for example, excessive worrying, pacing, hand-wringing or an inability to sit still*
- *Slowed thinking, speaking or body movements*
- *Feelings of worthlessness or guilt, fixating on past failures or blaming yourself for things that are not your responsibility*
- *Trouble thinking, concentrating, making decisions and remembering things*
- *Frequent thoughts of death, suicidal thoughts, suicide attempts or suicide*
- *Unexplained physical problems, such as back pain or headaches*

For some people, depression symptoms are so severe that it's obvious something isn't right. Other people feel generally miserable or unhappy without really knowing why.[3]

If you are experiencing these or similar symptoms, please seek the advice of a professional mental health care practitioner.

ACKNOWLEDGEMENTS

To my Lord Jesus Christ, to Him alone be all glory and honor.

And to the many people who suffer pain of heart or mind or soul.

The one true God, Father, Son and Holy Spirit, who has given me life and the talents to be able to write and serve Him and my fellow man.

My wife, Joyce, for her unwavering support during the course of this project and her willingness to be the frontline proofreader.

The pastors of the Northeast Circuit of the Rocky Mountain District of the Lutheran Church–Missouri Synod who asked me to create this resource and provided feedback.

Jennifer Fritzner for testing these devotions with some of her group counseling sessions.

Reverend Robert Miller, Kathy Murphy and Terri Tucker for offering their feedback on some of the material.

Sarah Elton for serving as my preliminary editor.

Donna Pyle, author of *Quenched*, for her encouragement and advice.

The folks at Xulon Press for their guidance and help in making this book a reality.

ENDORSEMENT

Pastor Buethe's book of devotions, Masks, is a powerful and spiritual reminder to us about our everyday lives. Not only have I benefited from it personally but I have used it in an intensive group treatment program for adults with anxiety and depression. We have all found it to be hopeful as well as helpful. It is sure to be a useful guide to many.

~Jennifer T. Fritzler LCSW, Program Coordinator for the Intensive Outpatient Program at Colorado Plains Medical Center, Fort Morgan, Colorado

1. A DOUBLE-EDGED SWORD

Much of our society values politeness. We are taught from an early age to say "please," and "thank you." It doesn't matter if we actually feel thankful or want to ask politely. The situation insists on the behavior. Receiving a gift or a compliment requires a thank you. We are taught that our response has nothing to do with how we actually feel or what we want.

To a degree this is a good thing. Politeness keeps our social interactions running smoothly. Learning to say "please," and "thank you," and similar behaviors teaches us to consider other people and not just ourselves. But it can also teach us to ignore what we are experiencing and that feelings like anger, grief, sadness or loneliness should be suppressed or ignored.

Politeness training may end up convincing some that putting on a good face is ALWAYS better than letting your feelings be known. It's better to act like you are having fun rather than admitting you feel lonely in a crowded room. It's better to swallow your anger than to risk hurting someone's feelings. It's better to "stay strong" than to let the grief you are feeling be known to others.

These kinds of messages may help us feel safer or more in control in some settings, but they also build barriers between ourselves and the very people we want and need to help us through those tough times. The masks of calm, happy, secure or whatever other state we try to project prevents others from knowing who we truly are. The masks help us feel safer in social situations while simultaneously slipping us toward isolation from our support system.

In extreme cases, we might even feel as though we have managed to hide our true selves from God, thinking things like "If God knew what I was really like, He would never forgive me." But God DOES know, and He tells us so in Psalm 139 where David writes, "You know when I sit down and when I rise up; you discern my thoughts from afar. You search out my path and my lying down and are acquainted with all my ways." (v. 2-3)

The good news is that God knows all about you. He knows your actions, your words and even your thoughts. And in spite of your sinfulness, in spite of your shortcomings, in spite of your disobedience, He still loves you so much He sent His only Son, Jesus Christ, to be your Savior. He promises to be with you each and every day of your life through whatever circumstances you are dealing with. You don't need to hide behind a mask with God. You don't even have to be polite. He knows the pains you are experiencing and He is there to hold you as you go through them.

God is there for you through whatever you are experiencing. There is no need to pretend to be someone or something you are not. God knows you as you truly are and He provides for all your needs. He is there to lift you up out of the circumstances that plague you. He is there to give you strength to endure. Trust Him. Rely on Him. Pray to Him. Let Him into your life.

Suggested readings: Psalm 139:1-6, 23-24

2. SO MANY VOICES

In our culture full of electronic devices and print media, voices are constantly bombarding us. They tell us how we should dress, how we should smell, what car we should drive and a myriad of other things. The people in our lives–our family, friends, coworkers and acquaintances–add their voices to the throng making demands, requests and suggestions for our time and energy. Add to that the voices of our own needs, desires and other internal dialogs and we can be bombarded by a cacophony of noise, both internal and external.

With so many voices vying for our attention, which ones do we listen to?

Under normal circumstances, most of us can manage to sort through the voices and focus on the important ones, the necessary ones, or the ones that somehow seek to fulfill our desires. But when the circumstances of our lives are already putting a greater load than normal on our emotional, mental or even physical resources, attempting to sort through the chaos can be overwhelming and nearly impossible.

It may surprise you to find out this condition is not unique to today's society. Thousands of years ago Elijah was having a very similar problem. He had defeated the prophets of Baal and then, along with the people gathered to watch, killed over four hundred of them. This didn't set well with Queen Jezebel and she threatened Elijah's life.

Thinking he was standing alone against the ruling powers, Elijah fled to the mountains and hid in a cave. But even there, God was with him. God instructed him to leave the cave and stand on the mountainside. And while he stood there, a strong wind came and tore chunks off the side of the mountain. And the wind was followed by an earthquake, and the earthquake by a fire. But God wasn't in any of these powerful, showy displays. (1 Kings 19)

Only after things got quiet did Elijah hear a soft whisper speaking to him, and that whisper was the voice of God. God assured him he was not alone, that God was with him through all his trials. And thousands of other people were also there to stand with him against the evil that was happening in the land.

God is also with us through all our trials and troubles, but to hear His voice we need to find a time and a place to be quiet. While many of the other voices in our lives vie for our attention by being bold and loud, God's voice quietly comes to us through the Scriptures. And Jesus our Lord tells us, "My sheep hear my voice, and I know them, and they follow me." (John 10:27)

When the voices of the world threaten to overwhelm us, the best thing we can do is find a place to be quiet and seek that quiet whisper in the Scriptures, for our Lord is continually calling out to His sheep, ready to lead them through the chaos to green pastures and quiet waters.

Suggested readings: Psalm 23; John 10:1-18

3. THE ULTIMATE MASK

Masks are a fact of life. Some of them allow us to deal with people or situations we find difficult. Others allow us to hide our true selves from others. Some masks are beneficial as they help us through temporary rough places in our lives, while other masks isolate us and separate us from the very people who could help us and lend us support.

For the most part, the masks we wear are optional. They may make our lives flow more smoothly and they might make relationships less rocky, but if we really had to we could learn to live without them. Life might not be as simple or as enjoyable, but we could still find a way to make it through the days.

However, there is one mask we NEED to wear. There is no substitute for this particular mask. Nothing else can serve the same function. This oh-so-necessary mask is the righteousness of Christ. This mask is placed on you in your baptism. (Gal 3:27) Through baptism you put on Christ and His righteousness covers all your sins. When the Father looks at you He doesn't see your sins; He only sees the perfect righteousness of His Son.

This mask of Christ is wonderful news for you. It means forgiveness, reconciliation with God and everlasting life.

This may not solve your earthly troubles, but it gives you a source of peace and comfort. It gives you a place of rest in the arms of your Savior.

But being the sinners we are by our nature, we have a tendency to take this mask off and leave it behind. We want to pursue our own interests, even when they lead us away from our baptismal identity in Christ. Trusting our own ideas and our own will, we wander away from the righteousness Christ has given us through His own sacrifice.

But in His grace and mercy, Jesus continues to call you to come back. He seeks you out like a shepherd searching for lost sheep. And when you repent and stop following your own will He is there to put that mask of His purity and holiness firmly back in place on you.

Once Christ has placed His mask of righteousness on you, it's time to relax and trust Him. Forget about trying to be a "better Christian" by doing all the right things all the time. Give up on the notion of making God happy with you by trying harder or being good. For the sake of Christ, God is already happy with you. He has adopted you into His family and made you His child through baptism. If you trust Christ's suffering, death and resurrection to make you right with God that's all you need to be the best Christian you can be.

Jesus has already finished all that needs to be done. He said so on the cross. (John 19:30) All that is left for you is to trust, relax and rest in a peace rooted in the sure and certain hope of forgiveness and everlasting life.

Suggested Readings: Galatians 3:23-29

4. WHO AM I?

Who am I? Why am I here? What purpose do I serve? Nearly everyone wrestles with these questions at some time during their life. It's part of forming our identity. It tells us how and where we fit in the world. It helps us figure out our relationship with other people. So take just a moment to complete this next sentence.

I am _____.

Writing out a statement like this makes it more real. It's not just some ethereal thought floating around in our brain. Writing it down means we can examine it and think about it more concretely. We can evaluate whether or not it is true, and that's important because many of us carry around thoughts about who we are that are not based in reality.

Many of us have heard messages telling us we are fat or stupid or a loser or other uncomplimentary things. Those messages can come from family members, classmates, coworkers, television, magazines and even from ourselves. Over time those messages can shape who we believe ourselves to be, even if they are not true.

So how can we know what is true and what is not when it comes to defining ourselves? How do we sort out the masks we wear from the real person? Where can we start so we are sure what we have is the truth?

In John 17, Jesus prayers for His followers and as part of that prayer He said, *"Sanctify them in the truth; your word is truth."* (v. 17) God's Word is the solid truth to serve as our foundation. God will not lie to you, even to make you feel better. His Word gives us the truth of our sinfulness, but also the truth of God's grace and mercy for the sake of Christ.

The identity God gives to you is to be His son or daughter, adopted into His family through the blood of Christ and the waters of Holy Baptism. Through Christ you are set free from sin, free from guilt, free from condemnation. You no longer need to carry those burdens.

Your identity as a child of God is secure because even when we mess up, God is faithful. He loves us through thick and thin, through good and bad. And even when we walk away from Him He awaits our return with open arms.

Taking into consideration your relationship with God through Baptism and for the sake of Christ, maybe it's time to complete that sentence again.

I am _____.

Suggested readings: Romans 8:1-16

5. SUCCESSFUL OR FAITHFUL?

For most of us there comes a time (or many times) when we take a look at our lives and evaluate what we have done and where we have been. We take stock of our achievements and our failures, as well as a sense of how we have performed in general, and then compare them to some standard. We may choose to compare our accomplishments to those of family members, school classmates or others who work in the same field as we do.

The values of our nation tend to encourage us to compare ourselves to people who are the best in their fields, or at least the best we know. So many of the messages we hear tell us that if we are not at or near the top, then we are nothing. Some coaches are fond of pushing, pushing, pushing to be the best and anything less is communicated to be failure. Supervisors at work often set standards of excellence that are difficult to reach. Even within families, parents or siblings can create an atmosphere that says, "Either you're a winner or you're disgracing the family." If we hear enough of those messages they can become internalized so that even when no one else is saying we don't measure up, we say it to ourselves.

But are we using reasonable standards for our evaluation? Are we using standards God would agree with? Just what does God expect of us?

It may seem strange to us, but the Scriptures have very little to say about being successful in life, at least according to the world's standards. God's idea of success is tied to our faithfulness, faithfulness to follow His commands, faithfulness to seek His will, faithfulness to humble ourselves and give God the glory.

If you are faithful to the things God has given you to do in this life, then you are a success. And how do you know what things you should be doing? If you are a parent, those things include changing diapers, doing laundry, feeding your family and even cleaning toilets. If you are married, those things include being committed to your spouse through thick and thin, better or worse, richer or poorer. Faithfulness can mean helping your neighbor, volunteering in the community or visiting the sick.

Success according to God's definition lies in carrying out these seemingly mundane tasks attached to the roles He has given you in life. When you care for others you pass on the love God has already shown you in Christ, and in doing so you become a mask for God. In a sense, you become God's eyes, ears, hands, feet and mouth. He works through you and other believers to carry out His plans in this world.

Of course, sometimes we can't even manage to be faithful in doing these small mundane things. Sometimes we are too overwhelmed by other circumstances and the laundry doesn't get done, meals become a bowl of cereal and we can't find time to spare for anyone. It is for those times and for all our failures and shortcomings that we have Jesus. He lived a life of perfect faithfulness in our stead. Even as He was carrying out His mission for our salvation, He made time to feed people, to allow little children to gather around Him and even to supply wine for a wedding.

5. Successful or Faithful?

Through your baptism you have been united with Jesus and whatever is His has also become yours. His righteousness, His suffering and death, His resurrection, even His faithfulness in serving others are all yours through faith in Him as your Lord and Savior. Through Him you are freed of the pressures to be perfect or to become the "best." Through Christ you are free to take care of those mundane tasks in your life, not out of obligation, but as a small offering of your thankfulness for all He has already done for you.

Suggested Readings: John 15:1-17, Luke 10:38-42

6. REST IN PEACE

Sometimes all of the demands on our time and energy become too much. We reach the point where we wish the voices asking us to do things would just disappear, the to-do list staring us in the face would miraculously be completed, the phone calls, emails, tweets and texts would be silent and we could have even five or ten minutes of peace.

But those things rarely happen, at least all at the same time. And so we look for other ways to find peace – a long hot shower or soak in the tub with the bathroom door locked, a drive out in the country away from traffic and the chaos of the city, a couple of hours sitting in the dark in a movie theater. All these things and others can serve as break from the demands of our day-to-day lives. But sometimes we find it hard to justify taking the time away from our responsibilities. Somewhere, deep down inside our psyche, we keep telling ourselves we can handle it and if we can't handle it, then we must be a failure.

If we follow this line of thinking for too long we might even come to the conclusion that if we can't do it all and do it all well, then our friends and family might be better off without us. Feeling overwhelmed by demands and coming to this conclusion that defines us as failures has

6. Rest in Peace

led more than one person to at least consider ending their own life as they search for a way to have peace and rest. They may even believe taking their own life will somehow make life easier for the people who love them.

While this reasoning may make sense in some way to a person overwhelmed by life, it can lead to a decision that will multiply suffering and pain and heartache. The suicide of a loved one never makes life easier or simpler for friends or family. In fact, quite the opposite is true. It often makes them wonder what they could have done to prevent this tragedy. They question what they missed or how they might have contributed to the death of someone they loved.

There is a much better way to find that peaceful rest. Put your life in God's hands. Trust Him to care for you. He promises you peace that passes any human understanding if you turn your cares over to Him. (Phil 4:6-7)

In Psalm 4, David calls out to the Lord for relief from his distress with a certainty that he will be heard. We don't know what circumstances David was facing, but during his lifetime he faced many trials. At times he had to go into hiding and was on the run because people wanted to kill him. He lost his best friend, Jonathan, in a battle. His first child died in infancy and one of his sons led an open rebellion to overthrow him as king.

And yet, with all these troubles David still turns to God in confident faith that his prayers will be heard. He encourages us to turn to examine our own hearts and then to quietly trust the Lord. And then he recalls God's faithfulness to His promises, bringing more joy and peace to our hearts than anything we can find here on earth.

David concludes his song declaring his confidence that in the Lord, even in the face of whatever troubles he is experiencing, he can still lie down and get a peaceful night's sleep, resting in the arms of Christ.

Right now you may not have that kind of confidence in God. You may even wonder if He is even aware of you and your situation. But He has promised to always be there, to always look out for you and to always care for you. He has made you His child and, as any loving Father, He is concerned about the welfare of each and every one of His children.

The hard part is taking those first steps of trust. When it seems everything else has failed you, trusting anyone or anything isn't easy. But God is faithful. He never fails to keep His promises and He has promised to give you the things you need.

So take that first step. Hand your troubles and cares over to Him. You may even feel an almost instant lightening of the burden that is weighing you down once you do. And with God holding on to your troubles for you, you may be able to feel the same safety David did and finally lay down to a night of peaceful sleep.

Suggested readings: Psalm 4, Philippians 4:4-9

7. WHAT ARE YOU AFRAID OF?

This life is filled with unknowns. We don't know what will happen next week or tomorrow or even five minutes from now. We don't know if the person we like really likes us. We don't know how pleased the boss is with our job performance at any given moment. The list could go on and on. And often these unknowns cause us to be fearful. We begin imagining what might happen, what could happen. We worry about paying the bills and meeting deadlines and raising children properly. We worry about what people think about us, even people we don't know and will probably never see again.

All this worrying gets in the way of actually living our lives. Our mind is often somewhere else rather than paying attention to what is happening here and now. We find ourselves only half listening to conversations, not really paying attention to what our children or spouses are saying to us, sitting through events and only having a vague impression of what happened afterwards. Our focus on what might be, what could happen, is stealing our life from us little bits and pieces at a time.

Perhaps worse than that, our worrying is interfering with our ability to trust God. Through Isaiah God has told us, "And I will lead the blind in a way that they do not know, in paths that they have not known I will guide them. I will turn the darkness before them into light, the rough places into level ground. These are the things I do, and I do not forsake them." (Isa 42:16) But do we really believe that? Do we trust God's Word?

In this passage God tells you He will lead you down those paths unknown to you. There is no need to worry. He promises you He will bring light to the areas hidden by darkness and He will smooth out the rough places so they are safe to travel.

If your nature is to worry, it won't be easy to let go of the fretting. So start with one small aspect of your life and let go of the worries. Trust God with that one area of unknown possibilities and see if He doesn't bring you through it unscathed. Reflect and remember all the trials that He has already brought you through.

Look at Peter. He trusted Jesus enough to step out of a boat and walk on water. But once he had taken a few steps, he took his eyes off Jesus and started to pay attention to the wind and the waves. As his attention strayed onto worrisome circumstances he forgot about trusting Jesus. He became afraid and started to sink into the water. As Peter was sinking he cried out, "Lord, save me," and Jesus reached out to him and pulled him to safety on the boat.

Worry and fear only multiply your troubles, but trusting in God and trusting Jesus Christ as your Lord and Savior calms your fears and eases your worries. Let go of your worries and rest in His peace.

Suggested Readings: Matthew 14:22-33, Psalm 91

8. NOBODY WANTS ME

A familiar children's song starts out, "Nobody likes me, everybody hates me; Guess I'll go eat worms..." It's used to tease other children who complain about being left out or who are just generally feeling sorry for themselves. Of course, the fear of being chosen last or not being chosen at all is very real for school children. No one wants to be the person left standing there alone when teams are picked.

In many ways that same fear carries over to adulthood. We fear being rejected in a relationship or a job application or in many other situations. While for some, rejection is just an awkward moment when they aren't quite sure what to say or do, for others any kind of rejection is devastating.

Those who are devastated tend to translate any rejection in any setting into "Nobody likes me, everybody hates me..." When life seems to be collapsing around and upon you, it becomes difficult to separate one issue from another and to sort out which feelings fit which events. It all becomes one big jumbled mass of "stuff" with no definition or distinction.

The good news is that God always wants you. He always has wanted you, even since before He created the world. Before He ever laid the foundations of creation, He had already chosen you to be His own. Even then He already knew you completely. He knew your failures and your successes. He knew the moments of "lostness" you would experience and the moments of clarity. He knew the thoughts running through your mind, the words coming out of your mouth (even under your breath), the actions you would take, and He still chose you to be His own.

He delivered His choosing to you in Baptism when you received His name, the name of the Trinity—Father, Son and Holy Spirit. In that moment you also became an heir of God's eternal kingdom. You have an inheritance waiting for you that is grander than anything this world has to offer, an inheritance that cannot be touched by the events of this world.

God wants you to receive this inheritance so much that He even sacrificed His only Son, Jesus Christ, in order to pay the price. It is through Christ's blood, shed on the cross for you and for all sinners, that your inheritance is secured. Not even death can stand between you and God's kingdom as long as you trust Jesus as your Lord and Savior.

Because God has chosen you those lyrics "Nobody likes me, everybody hates me..." no longer need to be part of your life. You constantly live under God's grace. You are wanted and loved and cared for.

Suggested readings: Ephesians 1:3-14

9. SWALLOWING YOUR PRIDE

For some of us there are times in our lives when we feel confident and very sure of ourselves. We believe we know how things work and have a plan intended to make us wealthy or famous, or at least give us the lifestyle we dream of. People in our lives, people we usually trust, may try to warn us about the path we are taking. They may try to give us counsel to look more closely at the risks and possible obstacles. But, at least for the moment, we are bound and determined to follow the course we are sure will lead to our dreams and we ignore the offered advice.

For a while our plan may work, or at least seem to be working. We are living more or less the way we had imagined and really enjoying life. But then something changes or something unforeseen happens and suddenly our magnificent plan blows up in our face. Everything we had created or pursued seems to collapse in on itself and we are left with practically nothing. We may find ourselves near bankruptcy. What recently had been an enjoyable path now becomes nearly unbearable.

At times like that, perhaps the worst part is facing the people who had tried to warn us, the people who had encouraged us to avoid the path we chose. Some may be almost anxious to say, "I told you so." Others may show us contempt or pity. Our pride certainly hates those possibilities. It doesn't matter whether they are real or imagined, we really don't want to have to face people who might treat us in those ways.

But the issue usually is less about the other people and more about our pride. We don't like to admit we may have been wrong. Sometimes we need to suffer a lot and be brought really low before we are willing to humbly admit we made a mistake.

The familiar parable of the prodigal son is about a young man who found himself in just this position. After demanding his inheritance and then leaving home to live a life of extravagance, he found he had burned through all his money and had nothing left. He was a Jewish boy fighting with pigs for a share of their food. It was about as low as he could have fallen.

But then he remembered what it was like in his father's home. Even the servants lived better than he did. So he decided to swallow his pride and return home, begging for forgiveness and a position as a servant in the household. As he approached his home, his father not only came running out to meet him, but then threw a celebratory feast to welcome his son back into the family. The son discovered his fears were unfounded and his father's love could overcome the damage he had done to their relationship.

You may or may not have people like the father of the prodigal son in your life, people whose love for you is strong enough to extend enough grace to cover any hurt or conquer any trouble. But you most certainly have a heavenly Father who loves you more than you will ever understand. He loves you so much He sent His only Son to suffer and die for you so you can be forgiven and receive everlasting life. If you let go of your pride and admit your sins to your Father, He will forgive you and restore you to a position in His family.

Don't let your pride keep you isolated from God. Don't be condemned to eternity away from God because you are not willing to humbly repent. Leave your pride behind and humbly come to the foot of the cross. Ask your heavenly Father to forgive you and He will for the sake of Christ.

Suggested Readings: Luke 15:11-32

10. RE-LEARNING TO RECEIVE

"'Tis' better to give than to receive," is one of those ageless adages we have all heard. Most would agree it's not bad advice, especially when trying to teach our children to be generous, compassionate people. But as with many other rules about life, it is not an absolute standard. Circumstances in our lives can send us through cycles of being givers and then being receivers over and over again.

Unfortunately, some of us have learned to be givers so well, it's hard to become a receiver. When we are giving, we are in control of the situation. We might feel a certain sense of pride or accomplishment that we are able to help someone else.

But to be placed in a situation where we need someone else to help us upsets our sensibilities. We feel as though we have lost ground. We don't like being dependent on anyone else. We feel vulnerable at the mercy of another person's decisions. We might even wonder what receiving from this person is going to cost us in the long run because we have also learned "there's no such thing as a free lunch." And if we are willing to be honest with ourselves, our pride also gets in the way. We don't want to admit to anyone, not even to ourselves, that we can't handle everything life throws at us on our own.

10. Re-Learning to Receive

Of course, that's a ridiculous stance to take. No one is equipped to handle everything in life. And if we stop to think about it, it becomes really obvious. We regularly rely on mechanics, doctors, plumbers and truck drivers to provide us with services or deliver goods that we need. We are all dependent on each other, no matter how much we want to believe we are not. But that "I can do this myself" voice is strong and it can prevent us from letting others know we are in need of something they can provide. It can also prevent them from intervening when we aren't even aware we need help.

Our heavenly Father knows all about our prideful independent streak. He knows we need an example of how it should be done and even to do it for us. That is one of the reasons He sent His Son in human flesh to experience the trials and temptations we do, to feel the hunger, the thirst, the pain and even the fear that we do. We have a Lord and Savior who knows exactly what we are going through and He showed us how to receive as well as how to give.

Jesus received help from the angels after His forty days in the wilderness where Satan repeatedly tempted Him. He and His disciples received meals and lodging from people in many of the places they travelled. He received from a woman who washed His feet with her tears. He showed us there is nothing shameful in receiving. There is nothing demeaning in allowing another person to come alongside us when we are overwhelmed. In fact, as He was describing the Judgment, He said that when we receive assistance from another person, it allows that person to minister to Jesus. (Matt 25:31-46)

God almost always works through people. He rarely performs big showy miracles. Instead He uses the hands and tongues and feet and ears of those who follow Him.

He comes to you through the people who care about you and offer to help. And He comes to you through His Word with promises to care for you in all situations.

Suggested readings: Hebrews 4:14-16

11. FIRST THINGS SECOND, OR THIRD, OR...

How many projects or goals do we put on hold because we tell ourselves there is something else we need to finish first? Sometimes there are legitimate reasons for finishing A before starting B, but often it's just our way of putting off something we aren't sure we really want to do anyway.

"I really should get in better shape, but I have to get more organized first," or "I should do some cleaning, but I have some errands to run first." Sometimes this way of thinking delays us from doing things we know we need to do, and sometimes even prevents them from happening altogether.

Often we even apply this to minor things that we find tedious, continuing to put them off until they become major issues in our lives. Allowing trash to accumulate rather than taking it out, stacking mail or other items on the table or counters until we aren't sure if the counter still exists, letting dirty dishes and leftover food accumulate until it becomes a health hazard. None of these start out as a major problem and yet they can soon threaten our health and well-being if we continue to put off dealing with them.

When we are dealing with other major issues in our lives, some of these minor things become just one more piece of an overwhelming morass of to-dos that threaten to bury us. It doesn't matter that some tasks are small and very doable. They become indistinguishable from the overall situation. And instead of working on the small parts that are manageable, we convince ourselves that the big problems have to be solved first, thus adding more pressure to ourselves.

We even apply this kind of thinking to our relationship with God, telling ourselves something like, "I really should get back to church (or read my Bible more or pray more), but I need to get my life straightened out first," or "I really need to get closer to God, but I need to get (a particular sin) under control first." But those kinds of thoughts are the result of our flawed human reasoning; God has never said anything like that.

Instead, God tells you of the wonderful things He has done for you even though you are still thoroughly entrenched in your sins. He tells us, *"while you were a sinner, Christ died for you."* (Rom 5:8) God does not ask you to get your life straightened out before you come to Him. He does not ask you to go through some ritual or process before He will listen. He doesn't give you a to-do list that must be completed before you seek His forgiveness and restoration.

In His mercy, God sent His Son, Jesus Christ, to die for your forgiveness even when your life showed little or no indication of wanting anything to do with Him. Jesus shed His blood for you because you needed it, not because you deserved it. He sacrificed Himself for you because of His love for you and all mankind.

11. First Things Second, or Third, or...

Because of God's grace and mercy, you never have to wait in line for Him to hear your pleas. You never have to jump through hoops of preparation before you come to Him for His forgiveness. He is waiting for you to restore you and lift you up.

Suggested readings: Romans 5:6-11, Luke 15:11-32

12. WHY DOES IT HURT SO MUCH?

Pain is one of those common human experiences everyone goes through at one time or another. Whether it's a stubbed toe, a scraped knee, a broken limb, or a serious medical situation, every one of us has felt pain. We are also fairly good at recognizing when someone else is experiencing pain. To identify when someone may be experiencing pain, we gauge his facial expressions, the way he moves his body, and even the sounds he makes. And often that recognition leads to some sort of compassionate response, an offer to help, an "I'm sorry," or an accommodation of some sort.

But not all pain is so obvious. While emotional and mental pains don't necessarily have easily identifiable outward signs, that does not make them less real. These types of pain can be the result of suffering a loss, sudden changes in one's life, failure, being bullied, disparaging remarks from others, and a host of other reasons. Often no single reason exists, but rather, the pain is the cumulative effect of multiple events and situations.

The problem with emotional or mental pain is, since it's difficult to see, it can be difficult to take seriously, at least when one is looking at it from the outside. If you

12. Why Does It Hurt So Much?

are the one suffering this sort of pain, little doubt exists about its reality but sometimes the people who usually care about us most won't believe the pain even exists. They might consider us to be lazy or liars or a drama queen/king, adding to the pain already felt.

Unfortunately, pain is a part of the broken world we live in. It will be with us until Jesus returns and sets all things right. Until then, pain will be with us in one form or another. But God uses the pain in our lives to shape us as a potter shapes clay.

"Not only that, but we rejoice in our sufferings, knowing that suffering produces endurance, and endurance produces character, and character produces hope, and hope does not put us to shame, because God's love has been poured into our hearts through the Holy Spirit who has been given to us." Romans 5:3-5

If during your pain you rely on the Lord and His strength to sustain you, the end result is hope based on God's faithfulness to you, His faithfulness of being with you at all times just as He has promised and His faithfulness of supplying all you need each and every day.

And you are not alone in your suffering. All of creation is in pain as it waits for Jesus to return. (Rom 8:22-23) In the meantime, God has given you His Holy Spirit who prays with you and for you. Even when your pain makes it difficult for you to find the words for prayer, the Spirit provides them for you in wordless prayers.

Through God's faithfulness to you and the presence of the Holy Spirit in your life, even in the midst of pain you can still have hope–a hope based in God's promises of a better day to come, a hope that looks forward to Jesus' return, a hope that God puts so deeply in your soul nothing on this earth can touch it. Through God's faithfulness it is even possible at times to rejoice in your suffering through your trust in Him.

Suggested readings: Romans 5:1-5, Romans 8:18-30, Psalm 6

13. FOLLOW YOUR HEART?

"Follow your heart" is advice that seems to be permeating our society. It is proclaimed at high school and college graduation ceremonies. Self-help authors and speakers point to it as the key to happiness and self-fulfillment. Theologians and spiritual gurus claim it is the only sure way to find God or "the divine" or whatever their type of spirituality calls for.

"Follow your heart." It certainly sounds good, and it at least seems to make sense. After all, how can a person ever be happy if he are not pursuing the desires of his heart?

But let's stop and take a look at the real world. Does following one's heart always lead to happiness and fulfillment? How many women are in relationships with abusive men because their hearts told them this was "the one?" How many people have been fleeced out of large sums of money because their hearts told them, "This is a good person?" How many new college graduates have difficulty finding a job because the major their heart led them to has little real world application?

Our hearts are notoriously bad at leading us on the right path to success or happiness or fulfillment. We can see that in our own experiences, but we have a much more reliable basis for not trusting our hearts. God's Word tells us, "out of the heart comes evil thoughts, murder, adultery, sexual immorality, theft, false witness, slander." (Matt 15:19)

As fallen sinners in a broken world, our hearts are just as messed up as everything else. What our hearts feel and our senses perceive and our minds contemplate are all skewed by our sinful natures. None of them can be fully trusted to guide us to the right path. It's hard to believe that we can't trust what our mind, body and heart are telling us but it's true. The book of Proverbs tells us TWICE, "There is a way that seems right to a man, but its end is the way to death." (Prov 14:12 and 16:25)

So if we can't trust ourselves, our perceptions, feelings and judgments, who or what can we trust? How can we ever make a decision with any confidence? How can we possibly find the path to happiness or fulfillment?

Unfortunately, there is no easy answer, no "one size fits all" response for all those decisions and situations you face, but prayer is always a good place to start. Rather than focusing on your own wants and fears, start with your relationship with your heavenly Father. Ask Him for His guidance in your decision and seek His comfort and peace as you go through the process of making your choice.

Your Lord's heart and will are more reliable than your own. He always knows what is best for you even when it doesn't agree with what you think is best. And even when you make poor choices, He can still make it work for you good in the long run, as long as you trust Him and seek His will for your life. (Rom 8:28)

13. Follow Your Heart?

If you trust Jesus Christ as your Savior and allow Him to guide your ways, you can be assured that in the end you will spend eternity with Him in Paradise. There is no IF with that hope, only a WHEN, for it is based on the promises of God and the sacrifice of your Savior.

Suggested Readings: Psalm 31, Psalm 73:24-28

14. I NEED TO BE STRONG

Often when a crisis hits, the people within the family react in a variety of ways. Some become confused. Others melt down into an emotional puddle. Still others are stunned into inaction by the shock of the situation and others put on that "stiff upper lip" and act as though nothing unusual has happened.

If it is in our nature to be compassionate or a caretaker, we might hear part of our mind calling us to be strong in the face of the crisis. We see others not coping well, not doing the things that need to be done to deal with whatever the crisis is and we think, "Someone needs to do this so I guess it has to be me." And so we stuff our own reactions to the situation to the back of our mind and our heart. Even as a soldier would prepare himself for battle, we feel the need to be bold and brave, fighting the circumstances or crisis at hand.

Being strong and taking charge of things can provide us with positive feedback. Other people might comment about how well we are dealing with the situation. We feel good about taking care of the people we love. We may even see aspects of the crisis become less overwhelming because the actions we have taken. Being strong strokes our ego and our pride. We might feel like a hero or maybe even a savior.

14. I Need to be Strong

But being strong has a downside too. It prevents us from acknowledging our own feelings, our grief, our frustration, our anger and other emotions. All of those are stuffed away where they won't interfere with being strong. In fact, being strong can become a mechanism to avoid the painful task of working through those feelings. And while we can keep them stuffed away for a while, sometimes even a long while, eventually they begin to wear us down and affect the way we deal with other people and situations.

Despite our reasoning that says, "Be strong," Jesus showed us exactly the opposite response to the death of His friend, Lazarus. When He arrived at His friends' home, Jesus was met by two grieving sisters who even told Him that He could have stopped Lazarus from dying if He had been there. Jesus could have taken the "I need to be strong" path, but instead He lets His emotions show and the tears flow.

But it isn't just Jesus' example directing us to avoid the "be strong" response to problems. God had given St. Paul a thorn in the flesh to keep him humble. Paul pleaded with God three times to take this thorn away, but God's response was, "My grace is sufficient for you, for my power is made perfect in weakness." (2 Cor 12:9)

Your heavenly Father already knows the feelings you are covering up and the mask you wear disguised as strength. When you acknowledge your weakness and seek God's grace, His power lifts you up and comforts you. When you acknowledge your own failings and humbly come to Him, His grace delivers forgiveness to you. When you acknowledge that sometimes the world throws more at you than you can handle on your own, He is there walking beside you, holding you up and carrying you through to the other side. When you admit that you are

Masks

too weak to bear the load, God shows you His strength and His faithfulness.

Suggested readings: 2 Corinthians 12:1-10, John 11:1-44

15. LOSING SOME WEIGHT

Healthy living, fitness and weight loss are all huge enterprises in our society. Nearly everywhere you look, some food or food supplement or fitness program is being promoted. And staying healthy is certainly a good and God-pleasing goal. In addition to the benefits of feeling good and looking attractive, it is part of being a good steward of the life He has given us. But not all weight is measured in pounds and inches.

Many people are carrying a huge burden of extra weight that no one can see. They are carrying the weight of many worries and concerns, worries about family members, about their jobs, about finances and about dozens of other things. This weight of worry drags them down and makes life more of a burden than a joy.

While certain levels of worry or concern can make us more effective in getting tasks completed, too much worry can have exactly the opposite affect. Excessive worrying can affect us emotionally, mentally and physically causing issues at home and at work. It can disrupt our sleep and make us more sensitive to criticism. Ongoing, high levels of worry can drain our energy and our motivation. It can cause heart symptoms and sleep disruptions and physical manifestations. In other words, worrying too much can be harmful to our physical health as well as our emotional and mental well being.

So what's a person to do? Telling someone to stop worrying is neither helpful nor productive. If it were that easy most people would have stopped long ago. Some people seem to almost be hard-wired to worry and they wouldn't have the faintest idea of how to stop. And yet, even our Lord tells us worry is unproductive and a waste of time. He tells us worrying won't add a single hour to our lives. (Matt 6:27)

Jesus goes on to say worry is really a lack of faith, a lack of trust that God will take care of all our needs. There might even be a little pride involved if we think no one else can handle things the way they should be handled. But Scripture offers us an alternative: "[Cast] all your anxieties on Him, because He cares for you." (1 Pet 5:7)

Your heavenly Father offers to carry all your worries and anxieties for you and He promises to supply all you need for this life and for the next. He asks you to trust Him to care for you and He has already provided abundant evidence that He is trustworthy. He has given you life and breath and sustains them every day of your life. He has provided food and family and shelter.

Most importantly, He loves you and cares for you so much that He sent His own Son, Jesus Christ, to carry the weight of your sins to the cross. All of your sins, even worrying. Those burdens are no longer yours to weigh you down. Jesus set you free from the weight of guilt and worry so you can live in the joy of God's grace, mercy and provision for your life.

Suggested Reading: Matthew 6:25-34, Psalm 27

16. I CAN'T DO ANYTHING RIGHT!

From time to time, many of us get that feeling that no matter what we try to do, it doesn't come out the way we expected. The remodeling project turned out to be more complicated than we anticipated. That project at work seems to be taking two steps forward and one step back. The surprise we planned for a friend never really came together. Even the small things like doing the dishes or gardening or shaving or getting dressed don't seem to be going as smoothly as normal.

While we all make mistakes and have off days, if we are already overwhelmed by other circumstances those less-than-perfect events can easily become magnified in our minds. They can overshadow the things that went well (or at least went as expected) and drag us toward despair. Those magnified perceptions can also lead us to conclude there is no way out, no help to get us beyond our "wrongness," no one willing to lend a hand to someone who messes up everything she touches.

One solution, one that appeals to our need to be right, is simply to deny that any of it is our fault and instead decide that our problems are caused by other people or by circumstances outside of our control. And it might work for a while, but eventually reality will set back in and then we might feel even worse for having blamed the people around us for our own mistakes, which can lead us into a downward spiral of blaming ourselves, blaming others, feeling regret.

While God's Word certainly tells us that none of us are perfect and that we cannot save ourselves, His judgment is not one that leaves us cast aside and hopeless. Those feelings of wrongness are supposed to turn us toward God and to His solution for our sinfulness. They exist to show us how lost we are when we rely on ourselves and our abilities. Blaming ourselves or others for our own miserable state doesn't solve anything. It only serves to drive us toward despair and alienate us from those who are close to us.

The only real, lasting solution to our wrongness is Christ's rightness. Jesus, the Son of God and second person of the Trinity, was born as a fully human infant so that He might live a perfect life in your stead. From the time He was conceived until He ascended into heaven, He didn't do anything wrong–not one single thing! And Christ's rightness became yours when you were united with Him through your baptism. As baptized children of God, whatever is Christ's also becomes yours.

The only thing required of you is to recognize your wrongness and repent of your sins. Blaming ourselves only leads to despair. Blaming others flows out of our pride and self-centeredness. But repentance removes the burden of wrongness. The wrongness is taken away and replaced by the rightness of Jesus.

Covered with the rightness of Christ, you can have comfort and peace. Having received Christ's rightness, you are freed from blaming yourself or others. Christ's

16. I Can't Do Anything Right!

rightness, given to you, can change the way the world looks and how you relate to other people. Through His rightness, many things that are wrong in your life can be set right, and you can relax and be comforted in the arms of your Savior.

Suggested readings: Psalm 130, Psalm 6

17. DO, BE, DO, BE, DO?

How is your to-do list looking these days? Will it fit easily on a sticky note, or does it look more like the list a department store Santa would roll out as he hears the requests of the many children that visit him? Does it mostly stay small or at least manageable? Or does it seem to have taken on a life of its own, growing faster than you ever imagined?

While our calendars, to-do lists and personal organizers are supposed to be there to assist us with our lives, too often they seem to transform into monstrous taskmasters driving us to exhaustion and then demeaning us by showing us the things we have not completed. And then, from somewhere in the recesses of our minds a little voice comes forth telling us we have failed, and if we have failed we must be failures.

Somewhere, either from the voices of others or from our own internal dialogue, we have learned to attach our personal value to what we accomplish, to the things we do and to the act of doing. And driven by this need to do, we forget to be, to be who we truly are and to be whom God has made us.

In many cultures being is valued over doing, but not so much in Western societies. We rarely talk about just

17. Do, Be, Do, Be, Do?

being. After all, just being isn't efficient. It takes time away from doing. It stops us from accomplishing the things on our lists.

But what if... What if we took time to just be? To be ourselves? To be with other people? To be with God? It might prevent us from completing some tasks or making some appointments, but it also might bring down our blood pressure and our stress level. It might help us be more connected with other people and with God. It might allow us to relax and enjoy the blessings God has put in our lives.

God hasn't called you to be His doer. He hasn't given you a long list of tasks to complete. He has called you to BE His child. He adopted you through the waters of your baptism and made you His own. He asks that you BE in His Word, spending time reading it and meditating on it so you might BEcome closer to Him.

Through Jesus' blood, shed for you on the cross, God has made it possible for you to BE holy and righteous, not because of anything you have done, but through His grace and mercy poured out on you. And as you spend more time being with God through His Word and through worship and through the Sacraments, He fills you with more of His gifts. He forms you and shapes you to BE the person He intends you to BE.

Making a shift from doing to being isn't easy. In fact, it can make us quite uneasy about the things we believe we need to be doing. But give it a chance. More time being with God might show you that some of the things you were doing aren't nearly as urgent as you believed them to be. And maybe you might find that what you receive from being with God will fill you so much you don't need some of the things you were pursuing so vigorously.

Suggested readings: Luke 12:22-34

18. EVE SYNDROME

All of us suffer from Eve Syndrome to one degree or another. It's part of being sinners in a fallen world. Eve Syndrome is the condition where we can ignore all the great things in our lives and focus much of our attention on the things we can't or don't have. That's what happened to Eve during her encounter with the serpent in the Garden of Eden.

The serpent was a great salesman, pointing out all the things she would gain if she just ate the forbidden fruit. He said it would open her eyes so she would know good and evil. He said she would even be like God! It was a great sales pitch and Eve bought it. She forgot about all the blessings God had provided for her and Adam. She forgot she could eat from every other plant in the Garden. Her vision narrowed to that single tree and its fruit, the one whose fruit God had commanded them not to eat. And then she ate and it changed the world.

Isn't that just like us? We are surrounded by blessings from God—friends, family, shelter, clothes, health, the list of blessings go on and on. And yet we often spend much of our time and energy trying to get other stuff just because someone else has it or tells us we should have it. We buy into the advertising telling us our lives can't be complete unless we have this product or that service.

18. Eve Syndrome

And then we make decisions that in the long run make our lives more miserable. We spend money that really needed to be used for true necessities. We are taken in by someone's "get rich quick" scheme. Or we make ourselves miserable longing for things we know we can't afford.

It's all part of the Eve Syndrome, forgetting about the blessings we have and focusing on what we don't (and probably what we shouldn't) have. As sinful human beings it's part of who we are. Even John D. Rockefeller, one of the wealthiest men of his era, when asked how much money was enough responded with, "Just a little bit more." So even if we were to acquire all the things we think would make our lives better or happier, we would construct a new wish list of additional things we think we need. It's a never-ending cycle that keeps us constantly longing and discontent and leading us away from trusting God.

But there is hope in the account of Eve and the serpent. Even as God is pronouncing His judgment for mankind's disobedience, He gives the first (albeit vague) prophecy of a Savior to come. He proclaims a descendent of Eve will crush the head of the serpent, the first reference to Jesus defeating the devil through His suffering, death and resurrection.

The Eve Syndrome will be with you in some way until the day you die or until Jesus returns, but you can live in the assurance that Jesus has taken care of everything for your life beyond this world. Because of what Jesus has done you already have the biggest and best thing you could ever wish for...everlasting life.

Suggested Readings: 1 Timothy 6:6-10, Psalm 65:1-4, Psalm 145:14-21

19. GUILT

Guilt is one of those basic human emotions we all experience. We feel guilt when we know we have done something wrong. It's part of having God's Law written on our hearts. (Rom 2:15) His Law nudges us to try and keep us on track with God's will for our lives. But as with everything in this fallen world, guilt can be misused.

Some use guilt as a method to manipulate other people, the ads showing all the suffering children or animals and then asking for money, that friend or relative who tells you all their ills and troubles before asking you to help them with something. Some people seem to be masters at piling guilt on nearly anyone they interact with. And many accept it with no questions asked and end up carrying a burden that isn't really theirs.

But it's not just other people loading us up with guilt. Our own conscience, corrupted by sin, can add underserved guilt to our load. It might be something we did years ago. It might be something relatively recent. We've asked God to forgive us. We've confessed our sins in worship and heard the pastor speak God's Word of forgiveness. And yet we continue to feel guilt. For one reason or another those words of forgiveness don't seem to stick.

19. Guilt

The longer the guilt clings to us, the more it drives us to despair and to the sense that forgiveness can never truly be ours. We may try acts of penance, trying harder, doing more, treating others more kindly, serving more. But none of it makes any difference. The guilt persists and perhaps even grows deeper.

So what can you do to find forgiveness? Where can you go for peace?

There is no single answer for that, at least not in the specifics. But the best place to start is by going to your pastor. He is there to listen to you. He is the one who can hear the confession of your sins and the guilt that plagues you. And then he can assure you of God's forgiveness for the sake of Christ. If he deems it appropriate, he may even pronounce those words of forgiveness to you the same way he does in worship.

Knowing that your pastor has heard you confess your specific sins and still pronounce those words of forgiveness specifically to you, you can rest in the confidence that God has indeed forgiven you, no matter what the offense may be. No sin is too awful nor can they be too numerous to be forgiven when you come humbly to your heavenly Father through the blood of Christ.

But what if you still feel that guilt even after you confess to the pastor and he absolves you of your sins? First of all, that should be an indication telling you that your feelings are just wrong. That may be hard to accept, but it's true. Our feelings can easily misguide us if we allow them. Secondly, the Word of God is never wrong. It won't mislead you. Our Lord's promises are dependable and sure. If, through the pastor, He tells you your sins are forgiven, they most assuredly are.

Masks

Trust God and His words of promise and forgiveness. Go to the foot of the cross in repentance and humbleness. Then rest in the comfort of a loving God and forgiven sins.

Suggested reading: Psalm 103, 1 John 1:5-10

20. IT'S NOT FAIR!

How often have most of us said or at least thought those words: "It's not fair!" We tend to look at our own lives in comparison to others and then, using our own biased judgment, decide life hasn't been fair to us. It may be our health or our financial situation, our relationships or our employment situation, but we see others who appear to be in better circumstances and conclude we didn't get a fair deal.

We need to remember that appearances can be deceiving. The co-worker who received the promotion we thought we deserved may have sacrificed his relationship with his family in order to get it. The neighbor who seems to have it all may be deeply in debt and in danger of losing everything to creditors. We never know another person's situation as well as we know our own, and thus our judgments are likely flawed.

But more importantly, each of us has exactly what we need for our current life circumstances. How do we know that? Because our heavenly Father has told us it is true. Jesus tells us to look at the birds of the air and the grasses and flowers of the fields and see how they are taken care of by our Father in heaven. (Matt 6:25-33) And then He tells us that we are certainly more important to Him than those birds, grasses and flowers are.

Our problem is that we sometimes confuse the meanings of the words "fair" and "equal." God promises to give us all that we need for every day of our lives; He does not promise to give us an amount equal to any other particular person.

God treats us more fairly than any human being possibly can. He does not consider our wealth or poverty, our race, ethnicity or gender. In His eyes we are all on equal footing. We are all sinners in need of redemption and forgiveness. When we come before Him He always has time to listen to our prayers, concerns, confessions and praises. Each of us is equally important to Him.

And while God treats us fairly when it comes to our status before Him, in another sense He treats us very unfairly. If He were fair, we would receive the punishment we deserve for our sins. Forgiveness would not be available because, at least in human terms, that wouldn't be fair.

But God is so unfair that He sent His Son, Jesus Christ, to carry the burden of punishment for your sins. Jesus lived a perfect life never sinning, never making a single mistake, and then He willingly shouldered not only your sins but the sins of the entire world and carried them to the cross. He could have cried, "This isn't fair," but He loves you so much He willingly gave Himself up so that you might have forgiveness and eternal life.

Life won't ever be fair, but you have a Savior who has overcome the unfairness through His own sacrifice. Regardless of how circumstances appear in your life, you can be assured that you have something more precious than anything this world has to offer. You have a God who loves you, a Savior who died and rose again for you, and an everlasting life of perfect bliss awaiting you when Jesus returns.

Suggested readings: Romans 5:1-11

21. WHERE DO I BELONG?

A portion of our identity is formed by the groups or organizations we belong to–the military, a sports team, our family or various social groups. Being connected to a particular group helps set us apart from others. It gives us a unique peer group and a sense of belonging.

Each of these groups has a set of requirements or expectations they place on their members and only those who meet them can become part of the group. A sports team expects practice and teamwork. The military has expectations of fitness and obedience to the chain of command. Groups built around a hobby or interest expect members to be engaged in those things.

Trying to become a member of any of these groups without fitting the expectations can be awkward or even a complete disaster. But even when we do meet the main requirements of the group, we may still feel like we don't fit in, like we're still on the outside looking in.

Some can spend their entire life moving from one group to another, looking for a feeling of belonging without ever finding it. But if we listen to what our Lord says in His Word, there is no doubt about where we belong. He tells us "Fear not, for I have redeemed you; I have called you by name, you are mine." (Isa 43:1) and "You are not your own, you were bought with a price." (1 Cor 6:19-20)

Your heavenly Father purchased you with the blood of His Son, Jesus Christ. You belong to Him. And that belonging is not based on how you feel or what you experience. It is based on God's promises, which never fail.

This belonging is more complete and more intimate than any earthly relationship we can experience. The Bible describes it as being part of a body with Christ as the head. In baptism you were united with Christ (Rom 6:3-7) and that union is so complete that you share in the results of His crucifixion and His resurrection. By belonging to Christ your sins are forgiven and you can live in the promise and the reality of everlasting life.

There will be times when this seems hard to believe, times when the circumstances of your life seem incompatible with belonging to Jesus. You may wonder if some of your decisions or actions have invalidated your membership in the body of Christ. But God is faithful to His promises. He has claimed you as His own and that will never change. Your belonging is not based on how perfectly you live your life or fulfill your various roles. It is based on what Christ has done for you and on God claiming you as His own.

He is your heavenly Father and He is always ready for you to come home, to admit your mistakes and humbly ask for His forgiveness. There are no other hurdles to clear or hoops to jump through, just God's infinite grace and mercy delivered to you for the sake of Christ.

Suggested readings: Isaiah 43:1-7, Romans 6:3-11

22. STARTING OVER

From time to time we all have those days when we wish we could go back to bed and start over. On those days we seem to leave a path of destruction and failure in our path, broken appliances, missed appointments, near misses on the highway, interactions with others that seem to end with misunderstandings and damaged relationships. Sometimes it's not just a day we would like to begin again but a whole week or month or maybe even our entire life.

Of course, we know that can't really happen. We don't have genies to grant wishes or magic wands to wave or time machines to allow us to go back for a "do over." When life isn't going well we need to do our best to work through things. We need to strengthen relationships, work on problems and not dwell on events we have no control over.

But one area of our lives is an exception to this. We have one area where we truly can start over, our relationship with God. The Scriptures tell us, "Therefore, if anyone is in Christ, he is a new creation. The old has passed away; behold, the new has come." (2 Cor 5:17)

Isn't that great news!?!? No matter what you have done, no matter how badly the day is going, no matter how many times you have sinned, if you are in Christ the slate can be wiped clean and you can start over. If you confess your sins to God and repent (that is, intend to change how you do things) your relationship with God is restored. You are once again in good standing with your heavenly Father for the sake of Christ's suffering, death and resurrection.

Now, this won't fix the broken relationships or straighten out the disaster at work or clean up the aftermath of weeks of not cleaning up the house. But it does give you a place of rest. Through your restored relationship with God you have a place, even when there is no physical location, to find peace and comfort. And when you have a place of rest giving you peace and comfort it becomes less burdensome to deal with the rest of life.

Being a new creation in Christ gives you a safe starting place for tackling the other challenges in your life. You can rest in Him and rely on His strength as you put time and energy into getting parts of your life back on track. Knowing your status as a new creation before God rests entirely on the work of Christ and the power of the Holy Spirit frees you from at least one burden of guilt. It also removes the impossible task making a fresh start for yourself from your to-do list.

Through Christ you have been made new. You are at peace with God so you can let go of the old things and live in the hope of what is yet to come, everlasting life with Him in His kingdom. And when you are on that path, there is certainly no need to start over.

Suggested readings: John 3:1-6, Psalm 51

23. GREAT EXPECTATIONS

Reality often does not live up to our expectations. People we were counting on to carry out some task did not follow through. A new item we purchased turned out to be of lesser quality and performance than we had anticipated. A relationship in which we invested a lot of time and energy never bloomed to match our hopes and dreams.

When our expectations aren't met, we may feel angry or disappointed or even devastated. Those feelings usually are tied to how important the issue is and possibly to whom it was that disappointed us. When we are disappointed by an acquaintance or someone we don't really know, we may just chalk it up to experience and move on. But when someone we trusted fails to meet our expectations, it's often more difficult to move on. We might even feel betrayed.

But we may be treating the person unfairly. He may have failed to meet our expectations, but did he know what we were expecting? Did she make a commitment to us to take care of something? Or are our expectations based on wants or needs we just assumed were known? Did we fail to communicate what our expectations were?

Sometimes our expectations are not realistic because we have either neglected to make them known or we have misunderstood the intent of other people. This can even happen in our relationship with God. How often do we expect God to answer our prayers in exactly the way we want and according to our time schedule? How much do we count on things going well for us because Jesus Christ is our Lord and Savior? Are we expecting God to do things He never promised?

Jesus said things like "If anyone would come after me, let him deny himself and take up his cross daily and follow me," (Luke 9:23) and "If the world hates you, know that it has hated me before it hated you." (John 15:18) In other places, He promised that those who followed Him would face various trials and persecutions, possibly even death. He warned His disciples they might need to leave behind their families and homes for His sake. These are not the promises we like to focus on, and yet this is what we may face if we are disciples of Christ.

The good news is Jesus' last promise before He ascended into heaven was "I am with you always, to the end of the age." (Matt 28:20) So as you face various trials, be assured that Jesus is with you. When you experience disappointment because what you expected didn't come to pass, remember God sees the bigger picture as He gives you blessings and His timeline is not necessarily the same as yours.

Many of the blessings God has promised to you stretch beyond this life and into the life to come. This life may be filled with trials and disappointments and failures but through all of them, Jesus is there with you. Through His sacrifice on the cross you can live with the best expectation of all, everlasting life with Him. And there is no chance of being disappointed; Jesus' own resurrection

23. Great Expectations

is all the proof you need. He has promised to return and take you to a place He has been preparing for you.

Suggested readings: John 14:1-6

24. WHAT ARE YOU WORTH?

A quiet epidemic is happening in our culture. It's not something your doctor can diagnose or prescribe a treatment for because it has no physical cause. And yet it can lead to all sorts of ills with relationships, motivation, decision-making, and yes, at times even physical issues.

The epidemic we face is countless people who feel they have no value. The stereotype for "value-less" people is the skid row bum, the teen runaway who has already spent years working the streets, the person with mental health issues who has no home or family and so lives in the shadows of society. However, the feeling of being "value-less" isn't confined to these caricatures of people. Many who appear successful by the standards of our culture still feel as though they have little or no value.

From top executives in large businesses to stay-at-home moms, many of us live with daily doubts about our own value. We look at what we have accomplished and wonder if it really matters. Or we look at how much is left on our list of goals for the day or the week or for our lives and question whether we have done enough to really count for anything.

But our gauges for assessing our own value are all out of order. We look at what we have done or our position

24. What Are You Worth?

on some mythical ladder of success. We compare ourselves to what we imagine others have contributed and we find ourselves to be lacking. But is that really what it means to have value?

Look at Michelangelo's David or Da Vinci's Mona Lisa. What have they accomplished? They can't move or do anything except stand in a gallery or hang on a wall, and yet they are universally acknowledged to have great value. Where does that value come from? In both cases their value comes from the person who created them. Michelangelo and Da Vinci were both talented artists whose chisel or brush could create a masterpiece.

Another way of assessing the value of a great piece of art is by how much someone is willing to pay for it. These two pieces of art are unlikely to ever be sold, but many people would agree they are worth millions of dollars.

So how do we apply that to the value of human beings, to your value? You were created by God, and His skill and craftsmanship far exceed those of any human artist. Just take a little time and appreciate the intricacies of your own body, how your fingers work, how you convert food into energy and building materials for your body, how you can fight off countless attacks by bacteria and viruses. You are truly a marvel of creation far surpassing any work of art.

And what would you be worth at auction? Well, God sacrificed His only Son to buy you back from the darkness of this world. Jesus willingly gave up His life so that you could have a more abundant life both now and in eternity.

So where does that put your value? Off the scale!! You are so valuable that God spared nothing to have you as His own so that you might live with Him forever.

Suggested readings: Romans 8:31-39

25. THROUGH THE LOOKING GLASS

In *Through the Looking Glass,* Alice, of *Alice in Wonderland* fame, goes through a mirror and finds herself in a world where everything is backwards or at least very unusual. Characters from nursery rhymes come to life. Writing has to be held in front of a mirror to be read. And the pieces from a chessboard were running amok. In short, nothing worked the way it did in the real world.

To some degree we all live in a looking glass world. Adam and Eve ate from the forbidden tree and nothing has been the same since. The way we see the world, the way we expect it to work is often backwards or upside down from the way God intends it to be. Sin has corrupted our thoughts, emotions and even our perception of situations. And stress, anxiety or mental health issues can magnify this topsy-turvy view of the world.

In our sinful state we often see the rules God has given us as confining and overbearing. They interfere with how we would like to live our lives. We would like to get even with someone who has hurt us, but God says, "Vengeance is mine." (Deut 32:35) We would like to have a fling with that person we are attracted to, but Scripture states, "Let marriage be held in honor among all, and let the marriage bed be undefiled, for God will judge the sexually immoral and adulterous." (Heb 13:4) Many similar examples could be cited regarding lying, gossip, our attitudes toward worship and much more.

Following the rules that seem right to us and to the world put us upside down with God and deserving of His punishment. Fortunately, God does not follow our rules of fairness and justice. If He did we would all be bound for hell because we have all sinned and fallen short of God's requirement of perfection. (Matt 5:48, Rom 3:23) According to this world's standards of justice, each of us should receive the penalty for our sins, everlasting death and punishment in hell.

But God has another solution for justice. He sent His Son, Jesus Christ, to receive the sentence justice requires. Jesus shed His blood on the cross to satisfy the wrath of a just God, and so, when you are in Christ, you are no longer sentenced to receive that punishment. God has taken the first step in setting our upside down world right side up.

So yes, the world doesn't always make sense. It isn't always fair. The way we see things doesn't always match reality. Sometimes it's our perceptions that are at fault; sometimes it's the world's corruption being displayed. Either way, something is broken and needs to be fixed.

Jesus Christ is God's solution for setting the world right, not by fixing it but by making us a new creation. He has already begun that work in you because in your baptism you were born again. You became a new creation in Christ. Through Him you are able to see the brokenness of the world which others are blind to.

25. Through the Looking Glass

For now it will still be necessary to deal with a looking glass world, a world turned upside down by sin. But Jesus has promised He is returning and when He does He will usher in a new age, an eternal age, when all of creation will be restored to the perfection in which God originally formed it. Then everything will make sense. Everything will run according to God's perfect rules and all the confusion and frustration will be no more.

Suggested readings: 1 Corinthians 13:9-12, 1 Corinthians 1:18-31

26. HELP!!

Work was busy and exhausting, so you didn't get home on time. The dog took an opportunity to leave you a surprise that now needs to be cleaned up. The house is a mess. Every family member is running into the house and then heading back out to other commitments. Every phone call seems to be someone who wants a piece of your time or energy. And the people you usually count on when you need to vent or unwind are all busy dealing with their own crises.

How do you handle moments like that? Do you explode in frustration? Do you want to run away and hide? Do you wish someone would miraculously appear on the scene and bring order out of the chaos? Maybe all of the above?

This kind of chaotic day appears in nearly everyone's life from time to time. Some seem to handle it almost effortlessly, while many of us struggle, flounder or wonder if we can even survive.

In some ways we aren't all that different from Jesus' disciples. When a storm came up while they were sailing across the Sea of Galilee they panicked and thought they were going to die. These men had watched Jesus perform all kinds of miracles and they were still frightened

26. Help!!

and overwhelmed by this storm. Later, after Jesus' crucifixion, they seemed to lose all hope, gathering together behind locked doors because they feared for their lives.

In both cases Jesus calmed their fears. On the Sea of Galilee, they woke Him and He commanded the wind and the waves to, "Be still," (Mark 4:39) and the storm instantly obeyed His command. When the disciples were gathered in that locked room, the risen Jesus miraculously appeared in their midst and gave them His peace, not once but twice.

In both these instances, He reminded them of who He is, that He is the One who has authority over all creation and even over death. This peace He offered to the disciples is also for you. This peace is deeper and stronger than anything in this world, because it is grounded in a hope that reaches beyond this life. This peace is based on who you are and whose you are, a child of God purchased with the holy, precious blood of Jesus. And because of that identity, you have the certain hope of everlasting life with Christ and in that hope you can have peace no matter what circumstances you face in this life.

Sometimes it is difficult to remember that this peace is already yours. When the world seems to be unraveling around you, the peace Jesus speaks to you may feel like a fantasy with no substance. But remember that the words of your Savior are truth regardless of how we may feel. Our feelings can mislead us, but His promises are sure and certain.

When things are chaotic and out of control, look to Jesus for His peace. He has promised peace to all His disciples and that includes you. Allow His peace to fill you and find comfort in His presence, even when your world is anything but peaceful.

Suggested Readings: Mark 8:35-41, John 14:27-28, John 20:19-21, Psalm 16

27. WHAT IF...?

What if I lose my job? What if one of the kids gets sick and I have to take more time off work? What if that spot the doctor found turns out to be something serious? What if I'm injured and can't work anymore?

What if...? We all live with those two words to some degree. We prepare for those contingencies that pop up as we navigate life. We keep a spare tire with our vehicle in case we have a flat. We don't wait until we have a headache to buy some sort of analgesic; instead we keep some on hand just in case.

But we can't prepare for EVERY possible situation. There are just too many of them. If we try to contemplate all the "what ifs" life might throw at us, it can lead to a sort of paralysis. We start to believe we have to have it all figured out. It can get to the point that leaving the house without all the answers becomes a frightening proposition. So we stay home, more and more afraid of facing the world because something unexpected, something we can't control, might happen.

And isn't that really what we want when we are trying to figure out every situation? We want to know we will be in control, at least of our own reaction, no matter what happens. We're afraid of what others might think of us if we don't behave in the way we want to be seen. It isn't necessarily the situation itself we are fearful of, but rather how we will handle it. We don't want to appear weak or confused or silly. We want to look like we have it all together regardless of what the world throws at us.

This need for control is in stark contrast to what Jesus teaches in the Sermon on the Mount. He says, "do not be anxious about your life..." (Matt 6:25) Don't be anxious. Don't worry about the what ifs. Don't be concerned about keeping everything under control. Why? Because God is already taking care of everything for you. He is already in control.

Jesus tells you to look at the birds of the air or the flowers of the field and how graciously your heavenly Father cares for them. He even gently chastises you about your worrying, "And which of you by being anxious can add a single hour to his span of life?" (Matt 6:27)

In the end, our anxiety about what ifs and our need for control are symptoms of our lack in trust of our heavenly Father. Deep down we don't really trust Him to take care of us, at least not without some help or input from us. But our Lord encourages you to look at how carefree the birds and flowers are. They fly and bloom without a care in the world because they are in God's care.

You are certainly worth more than birds or flowers. Jesus says that very thing by using a rhetorical question, "Are you not of more value than they?" (Matt 6:26) So trust God with your life. He's already taking care of you in so many ways, giving you life, food, shelter and so much more. And His care for you stretches beyond this life and into the next, having given you faith, forgiveness and everlasting life for the sake of His Son, Jesus Christ.

Suggested Readings: Matthew 6:25-34, Psalm 40: 1-8

28. URGENT OR IMPORTANT?

Every day presents us with a list of tasks to be done–paying bills, running errands, appointments, the list goes on and on. Our days become a merry-go-round of running from one thing to the next. Some of the tasks are urgent, or at least present themselves as urgent, such as tasks with deadlines, schedules for sports teams and things that pop up at the last minute. Urgent things demand our attention now! They don't appear to be something we can put off, and so they also tend to raise our stress level and add to the feeling of being rushed.

Important things, on the other hand, can often be put off until a more convenient time. We'll spend more time with the kids later. When things slow down we can go visit old friends we haven't seen in...how long has it been now? We'll get back to church when we aren't so tired and need Sundays to sleep in.

The most important aspects of our life are long-term commitments to people or organizations or even God. When we look at the urgent tasks and compare them to the important tasks, the urgent ones appear to need our attention immediately while the important will still be there tomorrow, or next week, or next month. After all, our spouse and children will still be there. Those organizations to which we belong are not going to disappear overnight. And God certainly isn't going to vanish into oblivion.

But is that necessarily true? A car accident or a heart attack can take people from us in the blink of an eye. And while God isn't going anywhere, the longer we stay away from Him the more foreign He becomes to our lives and to our way of thinking and acting. And what if that car accident or heart attack were to happen to us?

Isaiah tells us to "seek the Lord while He may be found." (55:6) Putting our relationship with God on hold is dangerous, not because God is going away, but because we never know how much time we have. Our life may end suddenly or we may end up losing ourselves in other things and lose all interest in God.

But your heavenly Father is always waiting for you, longing for you to turn and come back. Just as the father of the prodigal son. He is not waiting to scold you or punish you, but to forgive you and welcome you back into the family. He wants you to focus on the important things in your life, the blessings and responsibilities He has given you. He wants you to have a full and joyous life full of those important relationships, especially the one with Jesus Christ.

This full and joyous life stands in stark contrast to a life driven by urgency. Such a life is filled with stress and little joy. It has no long-term relationships to rest in, no closeness to others or to God, only a maddening rush from one transient thing to another.

When you put the most important thing, trust in Jesus Christ, first and focus on it, it puts all the other issues in perspective. The urgent things no longer seem

28. Urgent or Important?

quite so urgent. The stressful things seem less stressful. And when Christ is first in your life it is easier to sort out the important aspects of your life, the relationships God has placed there for you. What was once chaotic and confusing gradually becomes more manageable and serene by keeping Christ as your central focus in life.

Suggested readings: Luke 15:11-32, Psalm 116

29. QUICKSAND

Sometimes life seems like a "one-step forward, two steps back" proposition. No matter how hard we try, no matter how often we think we are on the path to progress, we just keep losing ground. It's like we are in existential quicksand that is sucking us deeper and deeper into its grasp. This can be especially true if we also struggle with mental or emotional issues where we can't always trust our own thoughts.

This quicksand feeling is nothing new. King David dealt with the same feeling and wrote, "Save me, O God! For the waters have come up to my neck. I sink in deep mire, where there is no foothold; I have come into deep waters, and the flood sweeps over me." (Psa 69:1-2) He was being pursued by enemies and persecuted by adversaries. He was on the run with no place to rest, there was no place he could feel secure.

Our adversaries today are probably not armed men seeking to kill us, but that doesn't mean we feel less threatened. Depression and other mental health issues as well as stress, feelings of being overwhelmed or having numerous demands on our time and energy can magnify even small matters until they feel threatening to our well-being. We can find ourselves identifying with David's feeling of being "up to our neck" trying to meet all of our obligations.

29. Quicksand

But what are we to do? How can we escape the quicksand?

David starts by confessing to the Lord. "O God, you know my folly; the wrongs I have done are not hidden from you." (v. 8) Confession is always a good place to start as we go to our heavenly Father. No matter what kind of mess we are in, usually some responsibility lays at our own feet, poor decisions we have made, choosing the wrong people to hang out with, approaching situations with arrogance or some other poor attitude. So humbly confessing is always in order.

David's plea to God is that others be protected from being harmed because of his errors. (v. 6) Only then does he ask anything for himself. Even then, his petition for deliverance is offered in the meekest of terms, "At an acceptable time, O God, in the abundance of your steadfast love answer me in your saving faithfulness." (v. 13)

We can learn a lot from David. No matter how life is treating you, you should always come before our Lord in humble repentance. When you start with confession you are able to approach your heavenly Father in Christ and in His righteousness. And there, with Christ acting as Mediator, you can pour out all your prayers to a Father who has loved you since before the world began.

Peace is not found by working harder to overcome the circumstances of your life. Trying to escape the quicksand of the many expectations placed on you will rarely leave you feeling free. It is only in the humble submission to your Lord and Savior, Jesus Christ, that true freedom can be found. Only through Him will you find peace for you soul and hope for tomorrow.

Suggested Readings: Psalm 69

30. WHAT'S THE WORD?

Where do you first turn when you are in some kind of trouble or mess? Many of us look to our own resources first—our intelligence, our skills, our creativity. And if we can't fix the situation ourselves, our second tier of problem solving tactics may be to look to friends or family. Who do we know with the necessary skills or knowledge to shed some light on our circumstances? Maybe we turn to professionals like mechanics or doctors or counselors. Or maybe we just feel lost and have no idea where to turn.

Where does God fit in your usual approach to a crisis? Do you turn to Him first? Last? Or maybe not at all? For many people, prayer is not the first place they turn when they need help. It seems easier to remember more tangible resources when we are on the verge of panicking. But even if you do remember to turn to God in prayer, remember that's just the first step. Prayer is you talking to God, but do you allow Him to speak to you during tough times? Do you open your Bible and read what He has to say to you?

While prayer is certainly very important, isn't hearing from your Lord also important? His Word can speak comfort to you in trying times, strength when you are worn down, correction when you have strayed and forgiveness

30. What's the Word?

when you need restoration. In His Word you can find His promises for peace, safety and everlasting life, and most importantly the story of God's love for you shown through His Son, Jesus Christ.

In Isaiah, God tells us, "[My Word] shall not return to me empty, but it shall accomplish that which I purpose, and shall succeed in the thing for which I sent it." God's Word works on you and in you. It is "living and active." (Heb 4:12) God's Word will change you, but you need to give Him access to your life. You need to spend time reading the Scriptures in order for them to do their work.

Taking time to sit down for a while and read your Bible can be hard to do when your life is engulfed in chaos. It can be difficult to focus when the issues you are facing consume your thoughts. But if you desire God's influence in your life, you need to allow Him in and that happens primarily through His Word.

Amazingly, God did not settle for just giving us His written and spoken Word. He actually clothed that Word in flesh and sent Him to walk among us. (John 1:14) Jesus Christ is the Word made flesh. The Word that broke into human history and preached and taught and healed and comforted. The Incarnate Word that knows what it means to be human with all our troubles, temptations, needs and desires.

Jesus Christ changed human history and, more importantly, your future by being your substitute. He lived a perfect life in your stead and then received the consequences for your sins and failures. He did all this and more so you might live in peace and in hope, knowing that regardless of what other troubles may come into your life, He has already secured your eternal destiny. If you trust Him as your Lord and Savior and allow His

Masks

Word in your life so your faith can grow and stay strong, you can be confident of spending the rest of eternity in the blessed peace of His presence.

Suggested Readings: Isaiah 55:6-13, 2 Timothy 3:12-17, Hebrews 4:12-13

DEVOTIONAL THOUGHTS

~ For those times when there isn't enough time or
energy for a full devotion ~

Mistakes we have made or sins we committed early in our lives sometimes have a way of haunting us. They keep creeping back into our minds when we least expect it. Each time we feel newly convicted and guilt rises up within us. But that's not how God sees it. For the sake of Christ, He has forgotten your sins once you ask for forgiveness and He will remember them no more.

Psalm 25:7
Remember not the sins of my youth or my transgressions;
according to your steadfast love remember me, for the sake of your goodness, O LORD!

Sometimes it seems like the tears will never stop. We have cried out to God. We have sought comfort in various places and yet the tears continue. We may even begin to wonder if God even notices our sadness or grief. But in the Psalms we are assured that not only does He know about your tears, but He saves them and records them.

Psalm 56:8

You have kept count of my tossings;
put my tears in your bottle. Are they not in your book?

Peace is often hard to find as our lives and our thoughts are tossed about by circumstances. Sometimes it's because we are looking in the wrong places, looking for peace where there is no peace. The only sure source of peace is our Lord Jesus Christ. In Him we can find peace, both now and in eternity.

Isaiah 26:3-4
You keep him in perfect peace whose mind is stayed on
you, because he trusts in you.
*Trust in the L*ORD *forever, for the L*ORD *G*OD *is an ever-*
lasting rock.

In some circumstances it can be difficult to raise our praises to the Lord. When it seems everything and everyone has turned against us, what is there to sing praises about? Perhaps we can sing praise simply because He and He alone is God. And maybe praising God even when you don't feel like it is the first step toward a more joy-filled life.

Psalm 148:13
*Let them praise the name of the L*ORD*,*
for his name alone is exalted;
his majesty is above earth and heaven.

"The Lord will provide" seems almost to be a cliché, a few words falling easily off the tongue but with no real meaning. Where is the Lord's providence when calamity strikes? How is He providing as we go through tough times? Because we can't see the big picture as God can, it's hard to find answers to these and other questions. Trusting God and His promises is a key part of faith, trusting that He is with us in good times and in bad and He is always doing what is best for us.

Psalm 145:15-16
The eyes of all look to you,
and you give them their food in due season.
You open your hand;
you satisfy the desire of every living thing.

Sometimes we may wonder what is taking God so long to answer our prayers. We pray and pray and pray and wonder why there seems to be no response. We want a quick answer, especially when life's circumstances seem to be bearing down on us. But God knows our situation. He hears our prayers and is waiting for exactly the right time to provide exactly the right answer to our petitions. It may not be the answer we expected or come in the time frame we would prefer, but it will be the best answer for us and for our salvation.

Ecclesiastes 3:1
For everything there is a season,
and a time for every matter under heaven...

No one likes to feel weak. Weakness makes us feel vulnerable and out of control. Only through strength does success seem possible. However, God looks at it very differently. He encourages us to be weak and vulnerable, because in our weakness we learn to depend on Him. We realize how little we can do without Christ in our lives and through this God grows our faith and trust in Him.

2 Corinthians 12:9-10
But [the Lord] said to me, "My grace is sufficient for you, for my power is made perfect in weakness." Therefore I will boast all the more gladly of my weaknesses, so that the power of Christ may rest upon me. For the sake of Christ, then, I am content with weaknesses, insults, hardships, persecutions, and calamities. For when I am weak, then I am strong.

Sometimes we can be our own worst enemies. We make friends with the wrong crowd and continue to spend time with them even after we realize our mistake. It's not that we really want to continue in our old ways, but we just can't seem to find the energy or willpower to leave it behind. It is then we need to join David as he wrote Psalm 141.

Psalm 141: 3-4
*Set a guard, O L*ORD*, over my mouth;*
keep watch over the door of my lips!
Do not let my heart incline to any evil,
to busy myself with wicked deeds
in company with men who work iniquity,
and let me not eat of their delicacies!

Whether it is through our inattentiveness to what it going on around us or through our own conscious actions, sometimes we find ourselves in a bigger mess than we ever imagined possible. Everywhere we look we seem to be pinned in with only bad options on every side. We see no hope, no possibility of escape, and yet somehow we come out on the other side relatively unscathed. It isn't luck. It isn't some random set of coincidences. It is the steadfast love of God as He cares for His children.

Psalm 138:7-8
Though I walk in the midst of trouble,
you preserve my life;
you stretch out your hand against the wrath
of my enemies, and your right hand delivers me.
*The L*ORD *will fulfill his purpose for me;*
*your steadfast love, O L*ORD, *endures forever.*
Do not forsake the work of your hands.

With schedules packed to overflowing, the threat of exhaustion is very real. Certainly by the end of the day, and often much sooner, energy levels drop to the point where it can be difficult to think clearly. Where can we find refreshment? How can we renew our strength? By spending time with the Lord–time in quietness, time in prayer, time in the Word. In the Lord we can find rest and renewal, peace and comfort.

Isaiah 40:30-31
Even youths shall faint and be weary,
and young men shall fall exhausted;
*but they who wait for the L*ORD *shall renew their strength;*
they shall mount up with wings like eagles;
they shall run and not be weary;
they shall walk and not faint.

So often we want to believe God. We want to trust His promises. Big or small, from salvation in Christ to comfort for the grieving, we want to hang on tightly to every promise. But as life grinds us down day after day we find it increasingly difficult to trust God and take Him at His word. But God can help us with that. He strengthens our faith by coming to us in His Word and Sacraments. He comes in, with and under bread and wine and water, working to create and sustain our faith so that we might live under Him in His kingdom.

Mark 9:24b
I believe; help my unbelief!

We are used to things coming to an end. It's part of our daily existence. Relationships end. People die. Businesses close. All these things and more teach us to count on the eventual end of everything. But God doesn't fit into our normal rules. He always is and always will be there. His love for us and His faithfulness to us are more constant and enduring than anything we have ever encountered.

Lamentations 3:22-23
The steadfast love of the Lord never ceases;
his mercies never come to an end;
they are new every morning; great is your faithfulness.

Our tempers can get us into a lot of trouble. We start out frustrated or afraid and before we know it, our emotions flares up and turns into anger. But anger is never helpful. It shuts off parts of our brain. It prevents compromise or cooperation. And Jesus describes anger as committing murder in your heart. Slowing down our reaction can save us from making a situation worse. Listening more, waiting to speak our piece, and saying a little prayer as we wait can save us from heading down a path away from God and His righteousness.

James 1:19-20
Know this, my beloved brothers: let every person be quick to hear, slow to speak, slow to anger; for the anger of man does not produce the righteousness of God.

We like to be in control... to hold the power in our own hands. It helps us feel safe, secure in our ability to call the shots. But this is really just an illusion. We can never be in control of all the elements impacting a particular situation. And to believe we can sets us up for frustration and disappointment. It is much better to concede that God is the One in control of every situation. Nothing happens without His permission and He is always looking out for what is best for His children in Christ.

2 Corinthians 4:7
But we have this treasure in jars of clay, to show that the surpassing power belongs to God and not to us.

Sometimes all we are looking for is a little help. We know what we need to do but we can't quite pull things together to get started. Family and friends seem too busy or uninterested in giving us a hand and we feel at a loss for how to get rolling. It is during these times that we need to remember our Lord is there to help us. He may not be able to be hands on to help us complete a project, but He is there to provide us with a safe haven to which we can retreat, a quiet place to rest in His care and love.

Psalm 121:1-2
I lift up my eyes to the hills.
From where does my help come?
My help comes from the L*ORD*,
who made heaven and earth.

At times we can get a general feeling of angst. Worry, fear and dread threaten to overwhelm us but there is no clear source. It's just a feeling we have in the back of our mind overshadowing all we try to do. How can you combat feelings when you don't even know where they come from? Rather than wallow in self-pity or punish those around us with a surly attitude, we can cry out to the Lord for His deliverance, His comfort, His peace.

Psalm 6:2
Be gracious to me, O L*ORD*, *for I am languishing;*
heal me, O L*ORD*, *for my bones are troubled.*

Our old habits can sometimes be our worst enemies. We work hard to get free of them, but when life becomes stressful or chaotic we slip back into them because they feel comfortable, like an old shoe. The most dangerous are the habits of our favorite sins, sins that take us further and further away from our heavenly Father. Christ sacrificed His life to free us from our sins, and yet we consistently gravitate back toward them. He will provide us with the strength to stay away from these sins if we turn to Him when we are tempted to go back to our old ways.

Devotional Thoughts

Galatians 5:1
For freedom Christ has set us free; stand firm therefore, and do not submit again to a yoke of slavery.

ABOUT THE AUTHOR

Terry Buethe is the pastor of both St. John's Lutheran Church in Yuma, Colorado, and Trinity Lutheran Church in Akron, Colorado. In addition to a Master of Divinity degree, he also has master's degrees in Educational Psychology and Systematic Theology. Before attending seminary, he taught math in Lincoln, Nebraska.

Terry has been married to Joyce for thirty-four years. Though they have lived most of their lives in Nebraska, they have called Colorado home for the last four years. Their first child, Jared, was stillborn, but the Lord blessed them with two additional children, Chris, who is married to Kim, and Patty, who is married to Mike. All four are young adults of whom Terry and Joyce are proud. Chris and Kim have two boys, Jaxin and Elijah.

Besides his pastoral duties, Terry enjoys cooking, barbecuing and reading. Along the way he has dabbled in blacksmithing, stained glass and balloon sculptures.

END NOTES

1. http://www.who.int/mental_health/management/depression/flyer_depression_2012.pdf?ua=1

2. QuickStats: Prevalence of Current Depression Among Persons Aged 12 years and older, by Age Group and Sex – United States, National Health and Nutrition Examination Survey, 2007-2010; http://www.cdc.gov/mmwr/preview/mmwrhtml/mm6051a7.htm?s_cid=mm6051a7_w

3. http://www.mayoclinic.org/diseases-conditions/depression/basics/symptoms/con-20032977

☺

www.ingramcontent.com/pod-product-compliance
Ingram Content Group UK Ltd.
Pitfield, Milton Keynes, MK11 3LW, UK
UKHW041954230426
12048UKWH00008B/325